I0589763

HOW A CIVILIZATION BEGINS

M●UTHFEEL PRESS

HOW A CIVILIZATION BEGINS

BY RICHARD VARGAS

FOREWORD BY MARGARET RANDALL

MOUTHFEEL PRESS

EL PASO /HUNTSVILLE, TX

How a Civilization Begins

Copyright © Richard Vargas, 2022

All rights reserved. No part of this book may be reproduced in print, digital, or recorded form without written consent by the author or the publisher.

Cover photography by Barbara Byers

Cover design by Creative Gong, El Paso, TX

Mouthfeel Press is an indie press publishing works in English and Spanish by new and established authors. Our books are available through our website, our distributor Itasca, and at selected bookstores or through author's readings.

Contact Information:

info.mouthfeelbooks@gmail.com
www.mouthfeelbooks.com

Published in the United States, 2022

ISBN: 978-0-9967247-9-1

Library of Congress Control Number: 2022939079

First Printing
$16

MOUTHFEEL PRESS

Para mi familia,
the one i was born with,
and the one i found along the way.

ACKNOWLEDGMENTS

Several poems in this collection appeared as is, or in a slightly different version, either online or in print in the following publications, for which the author is most thankful.

Anti-Heroin Chic: "7 days after my sister's death"

Bombfire: "the 80s"

Chiron Review: "new normal 4/1/2020," "cheating," "economic recovery," "milagro #9"

Cultural Weekly: "Tito's carnitas," "a note to the young artists living in these days," "how a civilization begins"

Last Call, Chinaski!, Lummox Press: "a rejection from Death," "what would Buk do"

Lowriting: shots, rides & stories from the chicano soul, Broken Sword Publications: "A Father's Gift"

Puro Chicanx Writers of the 21st Century, Cutthroat, a Journal of the Arts: "Tito's carnitas"

Silver Birch Press: "i am still waiting in line," "i am waiting for a peace"

Stance on Dance: "we dance (after A.O.C.)"

The Asylum Floor 4: "a rejection from death," "my ex sends me an email," "what love is #2"

This Is Poetry, Volume III: Poets of the West, Citizens for Decent Literature: "economic recovery"

Trailer Park Quarterly: "outside the box"

Barrio Panther: "Desiree's Poem…Surf Lounge, 1996"

Truth to Power: Writers Respond to The Rhetoric of Hate And Fear, Cutthroat, a Journal of the Arts: "doing laundry the saturday after the election," "thanksgiving; a rebirth"

CONTENTS

iii.

iv.

FOREWORD

Certainly, there are a great many poets with unique and powerful voices whose work tends to get lost in the increasingly commercialized miasma of publishing and promotion that passes for culture in this country. As is true of those vying for political office, those who "win" must have connections, money, and an identity that is in demand. Any given moment may put a different group of people in the limelight. One day it pays to be Black or lesbian, another Native or transgender. Always, of course, it pays to be a white man, preferably with the aval of academia.

Richard Vargas is his own person. Born and raised in Compton, California, he came up seeped in the culture of his youth—the fresh beans and tender tortillas, the addict father and close families and cool lowriders—but with only a whisper of the language his parents carried in their veins. He suffered and delighted in the expectations of his gender, including the sense that a willing woman or couple of beers could sweep the blues away. He served in the military, graduated from an MFA program too late in life to reap its employment benefits, acquired a profound political sensibility, and kept on going back to the world for more.

Through it all, he writes poetry. Poems that have appeared in books such as *McLife* (2005), *American Jesus* (2007), *Guernica, revisited* (2014), and now *How a Civilization Begins*. Garrison Keillor read his poems on three separate occasions on the Writers' Almanac, the radio personality's daily literary feature on NPR. Vargas's work has also been in several important anthologies. He has also prophetically curated the work of others in his excellent poetry magazine, *The Más Tequila Review*. But none of this has been enough to lift his work out of the swamp of the not-quite-well-known, those few poets who make it big enough to figure in our contemporary poetic canon.

Which is a real shame because Richard is an exceptional poet, one who has honestly and passionately honed his voice as he makes his way through the last years of the twentieth and first of the twenty-first centuries. His childhood culture, awareness, and yearnings, as well as the gross indignities and frightening absurdities that surround us, all come together easily and brilliantly in his verse. He blends current events and personal anecdotes with memory and the secret knowledge that is evident when we are able to access the intersections of experience and cultural clarity. We read his poems and know what he knows, feel what he feels, whether we are woman, man, Black, Brown, Native, White, Queer, Immigrant, jaded or still capable of acknowledging what passes for civilization in our time.

Sometimes, when reading Vargas, his use of language reminds me of Charles Bukowski in the 1960s and '70s. Bukowski's was repetitive to the point of vulgarity and, to my mind, often gratuitous. In Vargas's work, the same words fit effortlessly, taking the reader to where they live but never limited to some disconnected shock for shock's sake. His language is broad and inclusive, as often startlingly tender as brutal or speaking hard truth to power. Poems such as "patriot," "doing laundry the saturday after the election," and "economic recovery" move way beyond partisan politics to show us who we are at this moment in history. Poetic suites such as "blue," "red," and "yellow" are marvelous in their magical moments. The poem, "what I'm missing today" is particularly gripping as it moves backward in time. "the faux of july (albuquerque, nm)" is Vargas fully engaged with the landscape, making us see, feel, and smell it with him. "a rejection from death" shows his wry humor at its best, that humor is often present in his work and living in a place unique to him, somewhere between astonished expectation and irony.

This collection ends with Vargas's essay, "A Father's Gift." I am so glad he decided to include this text. I heard him read it years ago and remember the audience in heart-pounding silence when he'd finished; we were still inside his story, unable even to applaud until we'd been able to absorb what we'd just heard. Then we gave him a standing ovation. Coming upon it again now, I am tempted to suggest that those who read this book go to it first. It would definitely set a stage for the poems. But that would imply that the poems can't stand on their own. Not true. They do stand on their own, and eloquently. Vargas's choice to place the essay at the end was good. It completes this offering with a flourish, something like the "it's a wrap" uttered by a director who has just filmed a perfect scene.

Will *How a Civilization Begins* take Richard Vargas's work from that sea of semi-successful voices and place it where it belongs, at the very pinnacle of poetry speaking out of and for contemporary life? I hope so. At the very least, it will make a difference to all who read it, giving us new insights and many ah-ha moments.

Margaret Randall,
Albuquerque, spring 2021

i.

looking out

for Gerald Locklin

these days i start my sr. citizen mornings wrapping cold packs
in a damp dish rag and icing my bursitis-inflicted shoulders for
½ an hr. i imagine this is what it must have felt like the next
morning after trying to block Deacon Jones on a sunday
afternoon. i look shitty, hurt like hell, an offensive tackle
dragging my ass out of bed, heading into the kitchen in my
skivvies to grab a bag of frozen peas from the fridge, applying it
to sore purple bruises while sitting in the early a.m. quiet
replaying the game in my head. one play at a time. there would
always be a few "look out" blocks in the mix:

the only block left when my QB is looking downfield, arm
cocked, the second before releasing the ball as he strikes a pose
for next year's football card, but Deacon had just delivered one
helluva head slap. the ringing in my helmet distracts me
enough, allowing him to speed by me. i try to trip him, but he's
too fast, a mad bull making a beeline for the QB, who doesn't
have a clue what's coming from his blindside. times like these,
all i can do is yell, "Look out!"

i know he's one of the good ones when he picks himself up,
shrugs it off, removes the chunk of sod stuck in his facemask,
grits his teeth under the grimace of pain, gets a hand tucking his
shoulder pad back under his grass-stained jersey, huddles us up,
and calls the next play. he does all this while never giving me an
accusatory glance. that was you at your best, Gerry.

1

consider it a tribute that so many of your students have come and gone

leaving a trail of mediocre poems and a handful of good ones,

trying to conduct ourselves according to the example you set for us:

the beers and the cheerleaders are nice,

but in the end, having the guts to get up

after being knocked down

is all that really matters.

it's all about the poem

this is how it begins
except there is no beginning
there never was

be the blank sheet
of paper
crisp and clean
pure and unmarked

be still and quiet
as letters appear
to become words
becoming images
invoking feelings passing
thru the void

be the space
between the
lines and stanzas
be the infinite

there is no "i"

the "me" does not exist
only the empty vessel

the beauty of
this moment
is every time
this is read
the energy
expands beyond
itself

this is where it ends
except it never ends
be still
be quiet
it happens
it is

the day after a national emergency is declared

waking up a few minutes past 8 a.m.
i get up and go to the bathroom
then walk into the kitchen to grind coffee beans
and make my morning pot of organic french roast
i sit down in the living room with my books
briefly try to meditate but the traffic of thought
from the last 24 hrs is stuck in my head
like a freeway in Los Angeles on a friday afternoon
slower than a snail smoking a joint

i hear the young couple who live in the apt under
mine as they make muffled sounds back and forth
interspersed with a woman's lilted giggles
the kind that signals her arousal and receptive mood
i can't make out the words but it's the private give and take
couples make on a Saturday morning when they wake up
in the moment
together and alone under warm blankets smelling sweet
and familiar

five minutes pass before the tone of the muffled noise
drops an octave or two the way it does when passionate whispers
and body heat turn into the need to fuck

closing my eyes and leaning back into
my blue ikea reading chair
i ponder the passion they woke up to
the rolling rhythms they now ride
the soulful release they will share

when they are done
morning quiet returns
fills the room once again
i tiptoe into the kitchen
pour another cup of coffee
wondering where
does it all go
from here

isolated: taking a walk

walking the trails
at the nature preserve
down the street from where i live
on the first saturday of spring
still cold but the sun is out
an opportunity to stretch my legs
after spending all week inside
feeling like a hapless polar bear
adrift on a melting chunk of ice

the birds are calling back and forth
a bright red cardinal at the top of a tree
stands out in a landscape
of dark brown mud, gray tree bark,
prairie grass rising from the dead

standing on a small wooden bridge
over a pond of frigid water
watching geese rolling over
splashing and honking
preening their feathers
i hate geese because they are entitled

to shit everywhere they please
but today i will applaud
their annoying persistence

i see the young couple
with their two little girls
approaching from 50 yards
away singing a wholesome
song they probably learned
in bible school

the cardinal flies across the pond
to roost in a different tree
repeating the notes loud and clear
that announce his intent to procreate
and me, pondering our predicament
as a species that lost its way
that now stands on the brink

suddenly it is quiet
i'm in a vacuum of silence
so i turn my head and there
they are waiting for me
to vacate my position

the wife is whispering to her husband
the girls fidget and try to step forward
as the parents hold them back

i turn in the other direction
to give them the wide berth
needed to keep us safe
i walk off the bridge
to the sounds of the family
once again singing praise
and the hardy cardinal
determined to find
his mate

getting the mail

i decide to venture out
go downstairs and check the mail
(the hallway is Alfred Hitchcock creepy
that moment before the signature
soundtrack begins to pound
its eerie screeching pitch
into the ears of the audience
at the edge of their seats)
as my neighbors keep to themselves
behind their locked doors
watching porn or meditation
videos on their computers

would anyone hear me scream?

the mail consists of one postcard
from the feds reminding me what to do
to keep from getting infected
the postcard a miniature replica of the placard
the homophobe V.P. keeps waving in our face
on television during those conferences
when telling us what a great job

they are doing to keep us safe and well

i turn around and another tenant
is standing there waiting for me
to move away from the boxes
his depth perception sucks
because his 6 feet is more
like 3 feet and to make
it worse he doesn't look too good
face beet red
watery eyes
sniffles

i give him his space
walk back to my apt
thinking about the two
of us sharing the same air molecules

scrubbing my hands in the sink
like a doctor prepping for surgery
frantically searching for that bottle
of vinegar i bought last year
not remembering why
but glad i did while gargling
my throat squeaky clean

dying in a country that is great, again

the government invested heavily
in killing machines but not so much
in lifesaving machines
doctors will have to decide
which of us will be relegated
to breathe our last breath

the elderly and frail versus
a young breadwinner with
a family to feed versus
a wheelchair-bound paraplegic versus
a teen with a lot of life waiting to be lived
it's a class they don't teach
in med school
then the nurses will
give us whatever
feelgood drug is near
pull the plug and tubes
hold our hand so we
don't die alone

once it is done
they will check the roster
move on to the next bed
repeat the ritual
saving their tears for
shift's end when the brittle shell
cracks and the numbing red yolk
spills out and breaks

exhausted angels administer
mercy in hell by the dawn's early light
as our bodies stack up in refrigerated
trailers parked around back

patriot

the woman brandishes her poster
wears red, white, and blue
shows her grey roots to the camera
whines about being denied
her right to a dye job
while plopped in the passenger
seat of a pick-up truck
blocking the emergency entry
to the local hospital

new normal

one moment being absorbed in Netflix
a few seconds later looking out
a window while pulling my hair
a silent scream clings to
the walls of my throat

feeling warm fuzzies
watching celebrities repeat
madison ave slogans
from their well-stocked mansions
"we're in this together"
while fatigued nurses
line up on the state capitol steps
take a stand against
the flag-waving unmasked
foaming at the mouth

walking past parking lots
littered with blue masks
and latex gloves tossed
to the ground

the new used condoms
no one wants to touch

hands

the governors and the mayors
have been saying the same things
every day for over a month
their monotoned monologues effective
as a double dose of melatonin

it's only natural that eyes
drift over to their sidekicks
the person off to the side
whipping hands and digits
with lightning speed
contorting facial expressions
to emote the physical language
they share with their brethren
some look like maniacal
sunday morning preachers
in the midst of waking up
a still half-asleep congregation
and others are calm as a single
mom opening up and pulling in
a troubled child in need of comfort

they vary in color
size and shape
i wonder if they ever slip
toss in a "this person is so
full of bullshit, he/she just said…"

if i were doing the job
it would not be for long
because i would be tempted
to tell my version of the truth
until the hook was extended
from behind the curtain
pulling my ass off the stage
never to be seen again

4/1/2020

at noon the siren goes off
the one the city will use
to warn us to take cover
from approaching twisters
or nukes sent same day
delivery from an international
trading partner who is sick of our shit

it's lousy timing
considering the eggshells
we are all walking on
taking for granted
it is just a test
no longer an option

after a few minutes
someone turns it off
we stare out the window
hold our breath
and wait for something
to happen

the death of myths

now
at year zero we wear
dirty rags worn threadbare
sitting around a dying fire
littered with emptied cans
of soup and beans
blackened in the ashes

looking up at the heavens
mystified and afraid
left alone to build anew
we watch a shooting
star streak across

no one remembers how
to make a wish

what i'm missing today

2018
drinking coffee naked in bed
on a sunday morning
having heady talks
about parallel universes
bullshitting our way with a less
than minimal understanding
of quantum physics and wondering if
we knew each other in
a past life as i use a pillow
to block your needy cat
from trying to curl up in my lap
hoping you don't notice

2008
going up to my hotel room
after the poetry reading
at the community college
in Elgin making love as only
two starved people stuck
in sexless relationships
can and how you came

with a wicked grin
on the tip of my tongue

blooming into a field
of desert flowers
after a summer monsoon

1998
how your naked self
tiptoed in the dark of your bedroom
a statuette smooth as Greek marble
lithe and cool to the touch
retrieved the shiny black
leather belt from the closet
and held it out to me

prostrated yourself across my lap
whispered what you wanted me to do

1972
the time we were swimming
in Lake Elsinore under a full moon
when you glided into my arms
having slipped off your bikini

planted a kiss on my lips
that to this day still makes
me dizzy thinking about it
returning the favor
wiggled out of my swim trunks
two kids in high school
trying to make our parts
fit while underwater

ouch

how to talk to the sky

the language of no sound
is everywhere
it is in the dark brown soil moist
with the organic decomposed
that feed the tangled roots

the language of no sound
vibrates in every cell
passes through every atom
with ease like music
made when water slaps
the cold surface of stone

the language of no sound
rises up to the sun
the moon and the stars
where stories are told
recorded in time
with constellations
depicting gods, humans,
and beasts

doomed are those
who no longer
live in silence
who sleep behind
their walls of noise

blue

there is no perfect blue

because if you are singing it
then a bottle of rot gut whiskey
a loaded pistol and a faded
photo of someone you hate
to love is staring you in the face

because if you wear it
you will pay a high price
walking holy in sacred
knowledge through throngs
of the blind and ignorant
and weep as the ending
you predicted arrives
unnoticed

because if you smell it
you will pluck the petals
put them in your mouth
the sweet orgasm of your tongue
will make you shiver and swoon

close your eyes and when you wake up
the language you speak
will be strange and new

because if you dream it
someone is walking towards
you from far away
an old friend or enemy
it does not matter
what does is the key
they hold out to you
take it from their hands
use it to unlock the cell
in the prison
of your own
making

red

when you hear a cardinal's song
coming from a tree outside your window
it is a warning from your spirit guides
great change lies ahead
it will hurt

when your lover undresses before you
and the crimson panty floats down
around her dainty feet the same way
the velvet soft petal drops from a rose
what happens next will be better
than the birth of a poem from your lips

if the ant that stings you
hisses like a tiny flame
burning your flesh
its kiss is a reminder
to be grateful for being
able to feel

when your blood drips
from an open wound

let it fall upon a patch of dirt

or into a muddied pond

remember your origin story

whisper it to the trees and the wind

then lie down

and wait

yellow

when yellow is in your dream
it means you will be seduced
in the month of August
if you see yellow while awake
you are picking corn from a field
that does not belong to you
narrowly escaping the farmer's buckshot

when walking down an unfamiliar street
in a dicey neighborhood and you see
a yellow flower pushing through
a crack in the sidewalk
you will be protected
no one will harm you

when you crack open
an egg with a tan-colored shell
and the yolk is anything but yellow
it is going to be a bad day
best go back to bed
stay there

if you close your eyes
and see different shades of yellow
clinging to the back of your eyelids
your heart is being weighed against
the holy feather of the dead
now open them
your afterlife awaits

voyeur

i cut off the bottom
of a plastic bottle
filled it with bird seed
stuck it to my kitchen window
waited for over a week
nothing happened

this morning
pouring milk in my cheerios
looked up and there it was
light brown and red feathers
a sunflower seed cracking open
in her mango-orange beak

its tiny head crest
the always present
exclamation point
as she studied me through
the window's glass

1st time fishing (age 5)

mostly i remember reaching
into the bait bucket
watching the anchovies
swim away as i threw them
back into the water
my hands smelled funny
but i didn't care

someone saw a shark
prompting me to throw
a donut

we unwrapped the aluminum
foil and ate the burritos still warm
from my mom's stove
as a dead seagull floated by
going back towards the land
i hoped the shark wouldn't
get him

that evening i let my sisters
smell my hands and told them
about the shark that ate the donut
they made funny faces while
eating the rock cod but
i smothered mine in ketchup
it wasn't that bad until mom said
don't swallow any bones
they'll get caught in your throat
and choke you to death

Tito's carnitas

he was the only guy i ever knew who could survive the aftermath of WWIII with only a paper clip and a pair of shoestrings. he would have made any son a great dad but it was his fate to have 5 daughters who all liked to eat... a lot. my favorite story is 2nd hand, i wasn't there but have no doubt in my mind that it's true. after a weekend of hunting with his half-ass warrior friends, which usually meant plenty of booze, good weed, and a piss poor attempt to bring home some serious game, he was driving down a dirt road in his beat-up r.v. with his compadres in the back farting and sleeping, when out of the corner of his eye he saw a wild pig running parallel to the road, so he told someone in back to hand him his rifle and while pacing the pig and at the same time making sure he didn't drive into a ditch or a tree, he points his rifle out the window knowing he only has one shot. he squeezes the trigger, the pig flies head over heels, lands on its back dead in its tracks. he hit the brakes and jumped out with hunting knife in hand, started butchering it right there on the spot when the 3 guys chasing it down came upon Tito carving up their prize and one started talking shit until the doors to the r.v. swung open and out came 6 or 7 smelly hung-over hombres, each carrying a rifle locked and loaded. Tito gave the whiners a hunk of the carcass and told them to get lost. years later, after being out of touch, i ran into someone at a party who knew Tito with the 5 daughters. i asked how he was doing. the guy made the universal motion of doom, as if sticking a needle into his arm. i proceeded to numb myself with whatever was at the bar.

Tito's copper pot
cooks pork crisp, juicy inside
tacos from heaven

7 days after my sister's death

this morning i peeled and sliced
a potato into flat crooked rectangles
and uneven triangles
heated cooking oil and dropped
the pieces onto the hot pan
they fried until crispy brown
then i cracked 3 eggs
cooked over easy
the thick yellow-orange
yolks were intact
as they awaited the fork's
puncture that would
create the slow luxurious
release of thick liquid
over the slightly salted
fried potatoes

i warmed a flour tortilla
on the stove's open flame
flipping it over by hand
feeling the fire nip at
the tips of my fingers

and suddenly it comes to me:
if this were to be my last breakfast
i would die a happy man

dear sister, i hope it was like this
for you on the day you ate your last meal
i hope you smiled and thought to yourself
"damn, this is good"

i am waiting for a peace

not the piece they make
the rest of us fight over
a few crumbs tossed our way
over the walls of their gated communities
or from the balconies of an exclusive
high rise

i'm talking about
the pie with the flaky crust
delicate and buttery on the tongue
with the sweet and tart filling
made from fresh fruit picked
with expert care by dark calloused hands
belonging to people named
Juanita, Diego, Elena, or Jorge

i am waiting for a piece of the pie
with the silky-smooth filling
that melts in my mouth
the meringue or whipped
cream topping light and airy
as the taste of a summer cloud

providing shade for a wedding
or cover for an approaching drone

i am waiting to be seated
with people from all over the world
fellow human beings of all colors and faiths
the men, women, and children
exploited or murdered in my name

i am waiting for all of us
to be served a piece of the pie
the room suddenly quiet
and calm as the soothing smell
from the oven works its magic
we will take a bite and smile
a knowing glance passing back
and forth across the room
table to table

then suddenly
someone begins to sing
someone has a story to tell
or a poem to recite
we share the same language

laughing and crying together

until everyone agrees to start over from the beginning
the first time our tribes met and stood face to face
when it was all different and new

but this time
with pie

i am still waiting in line

only one employee is manning
a checkout-station as the rest
are closed off maybe for good

white haired, five feet tall at the most
stocky and wearing glasses thick
as the bottom of a coke bottle
the blue vest hanging over
her slumped shoulders
she could be someone's great-grandma
trying to stay afloat paying
property taxes on the farm
medical bills her dead husband
left behind or maybe she
likes the job because
it keeps her on her toes
and out of that dreaded
assisted living facility
her kids bring up every
time they come to visit

here she gets to meet people
who would normally ignore her
but they are now at her mercy
as she picks up one item
handles it with care turning
it over in her liver-spotted
hands looking for the universal
product code so she can scan and bag
she finds it soon enough
on her time, not ours
then goes on to the next item

the person she is checking out
has a shopping cart piled
high and i've run out of
tabloid headlines and lifestyle
magazine covers to entertain myself
i'm not going anywhere soon
there are two other customers
ahead of me and no one says
a thing or mutters a complaint
our minutes become molasses
dripping down a wall but worth
being a witness to the marvel
of her persistence

i am still waiting while
at the far end of the row
of vacant conveyor belts
and silent cash registers
the self-checkout is packed

people in a hurry
their time is so priceless
they rush to give it away

ii.

how a civilization begins

could you run fast enough
the first time you heard
the pop pop pop
so unlike the noise of deer
walking on dried leaves
or the splash a fish makes
leaping into the night air
for the low flying
mosquito

did you hide behind tree
or a big rock all day until
hunger or cold or both
gave you courage to
go back to the cave
where you found it scattered
all over the floor

did you pick it up
smell it
lick it
put it in
your mouth
light as snow
puffy as daffodil
crunchy like
a cricket

did you want to know
the secret
the trick
the magic

did you want
to make more?

we will never know

who was the man on the grassy knoll?
what was the color of J.Edgar Hoover's favorite pair of panties?
did the aliens give Ronald Reagan a butt probe,
and did he like it?

by now, we should be fine with all the stuff
we will never know
it was never meant for us
but for those rich white college guys
in secret fraternities who drink frog blood
and smear themselves with chicken guts
while dancing naked in secret rooms in the basement
where they determine future presidents
supreme court justices and senators
then roll dice for the women they will marry
hope she's not plain and comes from old money

and we
the common folk who will never know
should never know
would go insane if we did know
carry on our simple lives
poor and pissed
pay taxes and die
in ignorant bliss

education is

it's my sophomore year
finally made it to
the big show, so i'm
celebrating with the guys
standing in the shadows
passing around a bottle of strawberry
Boones Farm and a joint
during halftime of the
homecoming game when
they caught my attention

one of the vice principals
the short bald popular one
in charge of student activities
and the sexiest girl in the
senior class looking like
Deborah Kerr in her prime
wearing a pink cashmere sweater
and a skirt hugging her thighs
from here to eternity

there's a moon overhead
they are illuminated
like actors on a stage
he is giving her his father-
knows-best stance but
she's not having any of it
pouting and signaling

what she wants with
shoulders thrown back
hands on her hips

then he turns around
takes a step in my
direction cuz maybe
he sees me and maybe
he doesn't but before
i can say "run!" she
whispers something
prompting him to do
an about face
follow her lead
into the dark corridor

i felt a poke in the ribs
someone passed me
the bottle
i took a big swig
our team was getting
their asses kicked
no one cared

the F word

I.
my dad had recently overdosed
and moved on to junkie heaven
leaving it up to my mom to pull
me aside and have "the talk"
she told me in a low voice about how
sperm crawled out of daddies and
found their way inside mommies when
they were both asleep

she said there was a very bad word
for it, and she made me swear to never
say it ever, then she cast her eyes down
and whispered it

i felt privy to a secret handshake
as the questions i didn't know how
to ask slowly wrapped themselves
around my ten-year-old tongue

II.
later that year, while marching in single file
with my class at Mark Keppel elementary
we passed a group of 6th grade boys
i overheard one say to his friends how much
he'd like to F my teacher with the short blonde hair
green eyes and Mary-Tyler-Moore pointy boobs
i imagined them sleeping together while creepy
little things crawled from one to the other
under the warm blankets

III.
i finally discovered how good it felt to say the word
as an adolescent hanging out with the fellas while we
fantasized about being in a rock band or tried to score
some beer on a boring friday night
the sound of it leaving our lips gave us a swagger
made us feel mean, strong, and dangerous
the old man was now the F'n old man as our turn
raced towards us like a red mustang on a loose
gravel road

IV.
now i've lived long enough to know
there are different ways to F people
it can be done to them one at a time or to a large group all at once
it can be brought on by the simplest of gestures
a wink
a noda
smile
or it can be caused by doing nothing at all
the best F'ers become presidents and CEOs
i am neither

V.
finally
i don't use it as much
its shock value a thing of the past
my favorite word has evolved
into anytime a beautiful woman
looks me in the eye and says "yes"
and considering how often that happens
i'll just say my life resembles
the F word in the past tense

Chicano Viking, Paramount Jr. High, 1969

Henry Obregon was hardcore
a 9th grade loner with an icy gaze
and the quiet bulk of someone you just knew
you never wanted to run into in a dark alley

both local barrios
PV 13 and Dog Patch
knew enough to leave him alone
word had it that Henry kept a gun in his locker
on weekends he hung out with a real gang
from Montebello or somewhere in East L.A.
no one fucked with Henry
no one could figure out why he attended our school
and no one had the balls to ask

we were all surprised when
he showed up to try out for the football team
Henry didn't know the game but could run straight ahead
the way a fire plug shoots out of a cannon
a puff of fiery smoke in its aftermath
it always took more than two guys to take him down
he dragged them for every yard of open field
he could get until they pinned him under a mound
of sweaty, stinky moans and grunts
the sharp cracking sound made when helmets and pads

are thrown hard against each other announced
Henry hitting the dirt and weeds
of our sorry excuse for a football field
the cash-poor school district
had not watered for months

as his stocky legs
kept kicking and pushing him
forward for an extra inch or two
the coaches did the obvious
made him our starting fullback
even though Henry
never memorized
a single play

Ventura Espitia, our QB, would call the play in the
huddle, then look at Henry and tell him what hole to run
into, the numbered spaces between the center and the
guards, or the guards and the tackles. i was the left
guard, i shared the one hole with the center on my right
and the three hole with the tackle on my left. i learned
real quick that if Henry was carrying the ball
through the one or three hole, i better block fast
and hard, or prepare myself for the impact of
Henry's helmet blasting into my backside or his
cleats biting into my ankles and calves as he ran
over me. it only happened a couple of times. after

that i blocked for Henry with fierce desperation. no
lie, i would've made Vince Lombardi sit up and
take notice. we won more games than we lost.
Henry was our workhorse, our go-to guy when we
had to have 2-4 yards to keep the drive alive. after
the game, we would talk shit in the shower, the
sons of blue-collar families enjoying one glorious
and all-too-brief taste of what it felt like to be on
the winning side for a change.

last time i saw Henry
wearing pressed khakis
spotless white t-shirt
long sleeve Pendleton
draped over his arm
walking home alone
doing his warrior strut
down Rosecrans Ave

here's to Henry Obregon
a cold-looking vato
who knew how
to play a good
game of football

the 70s

after "Going to California" by Robert Plant and Jimmy Page

i feel for you, friend. you won't find her here. but before you are made to know that you will dance the senseless dance of a hundred disco nights and wear expensive clothes that look best on dept. store dummies. you will take lonely walks on streets where insipid eyes never meet or waste friday nights circling in endless freeway holding patterns searching for the right place to get off. when doing none of the above, you will sit in front of a loud tv, drinking, and smoking, all the time wishing you were somewhere else. then one night, desperation dripping from your pores like a cold sweat, you go to a place, pick a shapely woman wearing cheap lingerie, pay her to lead you to a cubicle with worn pillows and blankets on the floor, where she takes off your clothes, touches your penis. the dark void you will feel afterward will be the same as if you were standing alone on the moonlit beach, looking out at the Pacific Ocean, knowing the search ends here, there is no more.

the sound of the waves
a cold, bone shivering moan
you, an empty shell

the 80s

i was a warehouse supervisor for the Bristol Meyers
distribution center in Buena Park, flown into Dallas/Ft. Worth
for a weekend of meeting big shots from the home office in
Connecticut and sitting through boring presentations about
improved order picking techniques, safety in the workplace,
projected productivity stats. it was mind-fucking torture but i
sat there taking notes, looking serious and alert. it was a
corporate pony show. they were scoping the room for fresh
talent, the eager racehorses anticipating the open gate. but
some of us had other ideas, and at the first chance, we ditched
the evening's meet and greet with the director of this or the
V.P of that and hit the town with our peers that called the city
their home. they took us to Billy Bob's, the world's biggest
honky tonk, to watch drunk tourists paying to ride real bulls
as big as a VW. then we went to a club with obnoxious
flashing lights and fake fog creeping onto the dance floor. i
bought a few drinks for the perky blonde in our group who
worked for the company's operation in Chicago. we made it a
point to not talk shop and she agreed to a dance when
Madonna's video of Like a Virgin played on a 40 ft screen
while the place was abuzz with something about Too Tall
Jones and Tony Dorsett having just entered the VIP lounge. on
the way back to the hotel our host driving the car said she had
one more place to show us and then we were on an eerie
stretch of road, well-lit but not a car or soul in sight. she
stopped in the middle of the street and told us to get out, so i
opened the passenger door and stood there in the quiet early
a.m. in Dallas, Texas, as she pointed behind us and up at a
window in a tall bldg. and explained "that's where Oswald
was when he pulled the trigger."

a soft whisper said,
"there's lipstick on your collar."
i thought, "could be worse."

last word

you interrupted me
as i relaxed on the commode
and read my recently arrived
Esquire with George Clooney
on the cover for the umpteenth
time wearing a t-shirt
some guy in Italy designed
that would set me
back three paychecks

but you were too
busy thinking about
an evening of raunch
and revelry to notice
as i picked up the Raid
sprayed in your direction
watched as you sprinted
out of sight

this morning i pull back
the shower curtain
you greet me on your back
legs point up in the air
a fitting gesture of defeat

just as i'm about to pick
you up with a tissue
your limbs kick and twitch
making me jump back

giving you one last laugh
before your little heart
shuts down for good

i'll give you that one
it's the least i can do
as i take caution

poke you with
a used Q-tip
for good
measure

what would Buk do?

in bed she says she's going to leave
wishes she hadn't come over
feels unwanted

hindsight says i was supposed to
beg and plead for her to stay
but i'm thinking of the beer
and wine she's been drinking
since she got here when i ask
"baby, can you drive O.K.?"

she swings her legs over the side
sits up and spits out "fuck you"
then gets dressed and packs up
all her shit

her black border collie
the coolest dog i ever met
gives me her "what are you
gonna do?" look as she follows
her to their red Nissan

i stand on the front steps
in my robe watching her load
the car and slamming
the door as she gets in
and starts the engine

turning out the lights
i go back to bed
a night breeze comes
thru the open window
i hang a leg out from
under the sheet

it is cool and
feels good

1958 Vintage Valentine's Day Cards at the Antiques Roadshow

this is a set of vintage Valentine
cards from the 1950s
the kind of cards kids' moms
would buy to be passed out
to their kid's classmates on Valentine's Day
nowadays, they all have themes
based on the latest superhero
or Pixar movie
but back then, they were more
colorful and corny
coming in various sizes
biggest (i really really like you)
to minuscule (i have no idea who you are)

they were manufactured
by the JDL Press Co. in
Dinkford, Illinois, which was
started and owned by the late
Joseph "Dinky" Lundgren
in 1910 who made a fortune
printing pulp fiction paperbacks
never mind the inks they used
were highly toxic, and what they did
to the Dinkford River caused it
to catch fire in the infamous
River of Flame incident of 1934
that one cost Dinky almost all
the family fortune in political bribes
to keep him out of prison
and after it was all said and done
he turned the company over to
his sons and retired broken in spirit
and almost in wallet

the greeting card business
became a sideline that

took off when America
realized creating holidays
obligated people to spend
money on useless crap
in order to prove such
things as their love for
a spouse or parent
and their loyalty to
God and country

so the tradition of giving out
Valentine cards was encouraged
and cultivated as a healthy
and wholesome activity for children
of which there were many since
the G.I.'s returning from the war
had read Dinky's paperbacks loaded
with big-bosomed dames
and innuendo while holed up
in foxholes and flying bombing
missions, and they came home
chomping at the bit and ready
for the real thing

so there were a lot of kids
and money to be made
then and for years to come

now, introducing Valentine's Day
in the schools created a lot of stress
for the children back then
who usually had an idea
who would get the biggest
and mushiest card
it was their opportunity
to let that special boy or girl
know how much they
had the hots for them
even if they didn't know
what the hots meant

but that was the easy part
because once you designated
who would receive the biggest
card in the set
you had to decide who
would get the other biggest card
(there were always two)
and this required a lot of thought
you didn't want anyone getting
the wrong idea or creating confusion
in the mind of your true love
it had to be a safe selection
and as we all know now
when it comes to the affairs of the heart
being safe makes for the kind
of dull days that can lead to
a lifetime obsession with animal porn
or being tied up and peed on

it got even more complicated
since all the cards are geared
to a "will you be mine" mentality
which is a hard thing to give
to your friends of the same gender
little boys especially had
a hard time with this
even if you had "special" feelings
about some of your pals
you didn't want your best friend
in that kind of way
you just wanted to say thanks
for the new cuss words he
shared with you and how much
fun it was frying ants
with his magnifying glass
during recess

but now you had to hint at
a degree of want and implied lust
that included him and you and it was all
a complex uncomfortable mess
but the most dreaded part
was receiving a big Valentine card
from the ugly kid everyone avoided

at all costs or went out of their way
to tease and humiliate
or the creepy kid that wore the same
clothes day after day and would go
behind his favorite tree on the playground
and stay there until it was time to go back to class
that meant all along
when you imagined them
checking you out from across the room
well, they actually were
the next few days were spent
plotting how to turn that around
real quick
your reputation and standing
in the pecking order was at stake

thank you for bringing this in today
these cards are a true part of Americana
representing an age of innocence
and purity from which the country
never recovered

outside the box

not being able to find a job
in the university with my
brand new MFA degree
i tried doing the next best thing
to make ends meet
reading poetry at birthday parties

the first time i found myself
tied up and hanging from a tree limb
swaying back and forth
as someone jerked me up and down
while blindfolded adults swung
a Louisville slugger in my direction
me spouting off haikus
that rained down on the cursing
drunks like bite size Snickers
and Milky Ways

then they stood me up
against a wall
bent me over
pulled down my pants
blindfolded themselves again
as they proceeded to try
pinning my ass with a
sestina which was all good
until someone went to the garage
and brought back a staple gun

something tells me this isn't how
poet laureates get their start

my ex sends me an email

she wants me to pick up
all my shit i left behind
at her place
she's feeling disrespected
since reading my profile
on one of those internet
dating sites and can't
believe how quickly
i want to pick up the pieces
and get back in the game

she refuses to hear me
tell her how lonely i was
the last several months
we were together
how two people can occupy
the same space but still
be a million miles apart

she's a lovely woman
deserves to have what
i could not deliver
a guy who won't mind

sharing the bed with
dogs and a cat
and who actually knows
how to use every tool
in his kit let alone know
its proper name
who won't sit in front of
the tv watching an old
rap star chase a harem of
fame seeking hoochies and
scratch his head wondering
"why the fuck am i here?"
or picture his lungs turning
into a pair of dried prunes
from her secondhand smoke
and who won't mind taking the fall
for her weight gain when he
convinces her to quit

maybe if i'd just been better
in the sack we wouldn't
be here now

but there are some things
even i can't pull off

cheating

sitting outside partaking
nachos and beer at Kelly's
she looks at me and asks
"have you ever cheated?"

i recall stuffing paper money
under the monopoly board
in front of me when i was
a little kid making sure
Park Place would be mine
or how everyone in my
freshman honors english class
at Paramount Jr. High agreed
to write down beforehand
the passage from Julius Caesar
we were supposed to commit
to memory and copied it
during our mid-term
or how i took a short cut once
during a long-distance foot
race and didn't bat an eye
when the other guy
congratulated my win

but this isn't what
she wants to know
this woman who traveled
1300 miles to be at my side
this woman who crawls
into bed with me and

immediately puts popsicle
toes between my legs for warmth
then asks me to tell her a story
so she can fall asleep to
the sound of my voice

"have you ever cheated?"
she asks as she drinks her I.P.A.
her blue green eyes
scanning my face
looking for the
beginning of
a small crack

i can only hope
she doesn't see one

she whispers "don't leave me"

and we stay connected
me still inside her
shifting my weight
so she can breathe easy

the air in the room
is thick and primal
smells erogenous
drips down
the walls
with sticky
pleasure

just two lovers
in the dark
holding on
not going
anywhere

lying in our
wet spot
waiting for
the world
to end

Sunday morning, Los Duranes, New Mexico

I.

i get up and grind the beans
french roast aroma
calls her to come out
from under the blanket
and sit with me as we drink
in silence while a neighborhood
burro brays in the distance

II.

she showers as i start breakfast
a cheese omelet that turns
into scrambled eggs
while hash browns sprinkled with chopped
yellow bell pepper and purple onion
turn crispy brown on the grill

i slice tomatoes and a ripe avocado
to serve on the side with leftover
refried beans laced with serrano chiles
picked fresh from our garden

then i warm flour tortillas on the stove
pour us each a glass of orange juice
when she sneaks up on me
from behind and gives me a hug
presses her soft cheek
into the space between
my shoulder blades

III.

afterwards
she plays Patty Griffin on the stereo
a live recording of *Sweet Lorraine*
Lisa joins in, serenading me
from the living room
whilst i drag the razor through
white foam across my chin
the mirror reflecting the face
of a man beloved and at peace

milagro #9

after telling Lisa the only plant my maternal grandmother
cultivated was just outside her front porch and how every
time i was sick with one thing or another, i always got a cup of
hot mint tea, and the aroma was fresh and clean like right after
the rain stopped, so that no matter how shitty i felt, the tea
always left me feeling a little better than before, she comes
home the next day with a small potted mint plant for our
garden. the crisp scent of a leaf rolled between my fingers
makes dormant memories buried deep in my past flower and
bloom: my grandma's house in Compton where i climbed her
majestic fig tree as high as i could to that special branch where
i would sit and look out to see what i could see. the sticky juice
of red watermelon dripping down my chin on hot summer
days, and my aunt Dolores taking me across the railroad
tracks to buy me a bag of penny candy and the latest
Spiderman or Fantastic Four comic book.

healing memories
of grandma's mint-scented hands,
my love's gift to me.

Jazz poem for Georgia O'Keefe

after *Autumn Trees – The Maple, 1924*

colors layered

rhythms play
off each other

counter beats
so primeval
we   see sets
of stars

in the night sky
that burned out
eons ago
when we blossomed
under hot house suns

spread our petals
anticipating

an abundance
of possibilities
to come

how i wrecked my first car

we were parked in the back of
a local industrial park
half-naked teens in the front seat
putting the warm So. California
night to good use
a helicopter overhead shined
its spotlight on us
worse than a cold shower
we made a run for the open road
wanted to be invisible
didn't use headlights
didn't see the concrete curb
waiting for us dead
ahead like the iceberg
that sank the Titanic
fluids leaking everywhere
steering column bent crooked
a flat tire

cops pulled up
may day may day
we were going down

but she rose to the occasion
showed no hesitation as she opened
the door and stepped out
cooler than a cherry popsicle
approached the cop car

explained with a straight face
we got a flat on the road
pulled into the parking lot
to change the tire
thought it was the safe
thing to do
they nodded and left
then she turned around
started walking towards me

bright glow of a nearby streetlamp highlighting
the soft curves of her silhouette
bending over to kiss my swollen nose
whispering in my ear that my t-shirt
was inside out

Desiree's poem... Surf Lounge, 1996

i promised i'd write her a poem
a woman who could make
men do the stupid things
like start wars or beat up
their best friend
but all i can think of
is that king in the bible
who wasn't going to kill
John the Baptist until
Salome did her dance
on his lap and squirmed
down hard as she
nibbled his ear

her dark soft hair teasing
his flabby chest as bloodshot
eyes rolled back and he
whispered "yes...yes...yes!"

her price met
before he even knew
what it was

what love is #2
("I love you too, but not in that way...")

no sooner had the words
left her lips when
the sound system in the café
begins to churn out
the opening notes
to Bob Marley's "Waiting in Vain"
the bittersweet sound
of his voice coming to terms
with what will never be
while the flame in his heart
refuses to be snuffed out
makes my insides sink
down into the chasm
unfolding before me

wise men and women
throughout the ages
have told us the universe
is ruled by love
maybe
maybe not
all i know
is right now

on any given day
love can be
one cruel and cold
mother fucker

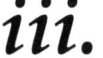

November 2016
doing laundry the saturday after the election

wondering if the numbing sensation
i wear these days like a second skin
will ever slough off
will i ever feel again

when on cue
as if she could read my thoughts
a stout and voluptuous black woman
standing at the table behind me
breaks out into song while folding
garments of all sizes from the several
piles of clothes rising before her

her sultry voice honed from a people's history
hanging from the wrong end of a rope
sings of being a motherless child
needing guidance from heaven
and a strong shoulder to lean on
during the dark days ahead

so it happens here
in the most unexpected of places
gospel and blues wrapping around
the cold dead space in my chest

transforming it into a warm shelter
for my anger to lie down and sleep

this is the part of the poem
where i'm supposed to praise
our ability to take a hard sucker punch
and carry on the good fight
but the reality is this pool
of sewage and shit we made
for ourselves is sucking me down
i'm choking on tears
yet to be formed

the words on the page of the book
i hold in my hands begin to blur
and slide off the paper

i pretend to continue reading

thanksgiving; a rebirth

no family meal
no friends and drink
laughter or lounging listless
on a soft sofa watching meaningless
football games

i walked to the edge of the Rock River
lit dried sage bundled and wrapped
in scarlet twine

faced south as smoke
encircled me under gray sky
and cold air embraced my bones
closed my eyes and prayed
asked that my brothers and sisters
protecting our water and lands
be safe from rubber bullets and grenades
water cannons and tear gas
i asked the spirit of the river
to come between them and
the corporate enforcer's intent

faced west and felt the sacred smoke
wash over me as i asked for strength
of heart and resolve of spirit to face the rising evil before us
to be worthy of the pain that awaits in the days ahead
asked for a shield of butterfly wings and a sword of feathers
arrows made of poems and song
sharp and straight

turned and faced north
thoughts and prayers sent to
comrades in arms
fellow veterans deploying to meet
the serpent of greed head on
plunging into combat with
the will of the warrior and the
heart of the peacemaker

finally i faced the east
grateful for this moment
my renewal of self
as i inhaled the surrounding smoke
and felt one with the calm
flow of the river
embracing me
bonding me to this land
and its people

i dropped the burning sage
my gratitude acknowledged
by the soft sound of water
meeting flame

7/4/19
the faux of July (Albuquerque, NM)

this year the Río Grande
is a brimming artery
pumping life into the
heart of this high desert land
where coyote scat dries
hard on a dusty dirt trail
in the late morning sun

at the water's edge
i set to fire the bundle
of sage carried in my hand
gently wave sacred smoke
around me through me

i turn to the west
where an ocean, almost
dead, spews up whales
with bellies full of plastic
and fish with glow-in-the-dark tumors
as radiation from across the sea
drips into the water and
no one gives a fuck

rotating
i turn to the north
hear the cracking of ancient
glaciers retreating while
floating ice caps break
into chunks clung to by
starving polar bears so lean
we can count their ribs
as we show our concern
by posting frowning emojis
on our Facebook

i face east where today
machines of war will be
displayed as a reminder
we are governed by those
who mock compassion
and good will towards
those in desperate need
governed by those who sow
seeds of hate and flaunt the sword
while the egos of the rich
gleam and shine
like the golden calf
they worship

facing the south
i can only weep

seeing the floating corpses
of a father and daughter
holding onto each other
together fleeing the horrors
and atrocities taking
over their homeland
fleeing into the hateful
clutches of an ugly people
ruled by fear who rip children
from the arms of parents
locking them up in cages
of genocidal dreams
and the toxic gasps
of a dying empire

today you can keep
your beer and hotdogs
your fireworks and
parades dripping
with phony flag waving
citizens who don't
know the words to
their precious anthems

today i will mourn
hang my head
heavy in shame
with tearful eyes

watch sage smoke
drift on currents
of wind rising into
an unforgiving sky

dropping the sage
into the river
my humble offering
the river spits
it back

the investment company's president visits the job

looks like she walked out of a Sears catalog
wearing a salmon-colored business suit
librarian glasses and conservative pumps
she carries a small purse over her shoulder
the internet estimates her net worth at 17.4 billion

an entourage runs interference
looking out for any unwelcome surprises
the workers at the staged workstations take calls
and try not to stare as she takes her seat to be briefed
by powerpoint presentations rehearsed for the last two weeks

the subtle stench of dirty dollar bills filling the room
a fart cloud that will linger for months

economic recovery

on the first day of training they
show us a video about the company's
global responsibility
how they go into third world countries
lock up their supply of the best coffee beans
show the locals better ways
to grow and harvest
increase output
decrease cost

they are green, too
convince governments that
their national parks can still
be cultivated without damaging
the pristine sheen of a fragile
and timeless subtropical forest

workers are provided with childcare
for the kids so papa and mama can
both work the beans
picking and processing
sunup to sundown

then we see a man
in the back of his simple home
proudly standing in front of an outhouse
he opens the door, and inside is
a commode, the kind that flushes
he is beaming and announces to
the camera in his native tongue

it makes him feel like he is one
of the rich people in his country
as a goat emits "baaaah-baaaaah"
in the background

a few weeks later
out of training and on the phone
i'm taking calls from my
fellow countrymen who complain
about how lousy their five-dollar
cup-of-joe tasted that morning
because it was too hot
or did not have the extra
caramel crunchies and whipped cream
they specified during their order
and when are we going
to have organic soy milk
available because if
we're not they are taking
their business elsewhere
and that kid you call
a barista needs to be
taught some goddamn manners
because they had to wait 10 minutes
to get their coffee which
made them late for work
and by the way doesn't
all this inconvenience entitle
them to some coupons for
free drinks?

the day isn't half over
already i have a killer headache
getting paid one dollar more
than the local minimum wage
to stroke a population that can't figure
out the right thing to do when
their kids are shot up
and massacred in the classroom
by gun toting lunatics

but has no problem finding
the time to call and bitch
about the real important
things in their lives

while the grateful worker
somewhere in Central America
is taking a leisurely dump in his
fancy toilet reading the
spanish edition of the
Wall Street Journal

cinco de mayo

everybody's Mexican
kiwi-mango flavored margaritas
chips made with organic non-GMO corn
mild salsa from Trader Joe's
designer tequilas costing
mucho dinero

everybody's Mexican
fake moustache
sombrero
guacamole and
oye como va

everybody's Mexican
job stealing drug dealers
rapists and criminals
no good for nothing
house-cleaning car-washing
lawn-mowing crop-picking
cooks and nannies

easy to be a Mexican
for just one day
hard to be a Mexican
24/7 in the USA

forgiveness

i will forgive your
raping of the innocents
the theft of their joys and hopes

i will forgive your
dumping of poisons into
air we breathe and water we drink

i will forgive your
profits of war as you turn pencils
and books into bullets

i will forgive your
hard heart of granite
outlawing the sharing of food
with the hungry poor

i will forgive your
hatreds and fears
for any of us who dare
be different from you

i will forgive
as the Buddha says
let go and walk away
to unchain my spirit
set free my thoughts
for my own ascension
to inner light and knowledge
but first let me spread my wings
one last time
unsheathe my sword
dive into this fray

afterwards
i will pay tribute to
our new beginning
paint one last bloody canvas
with a dark red sky
arrange your white bone chips
into a mosaic of doves
in mid-flight

let me give you the reason
you will need
to forgive me

breakfast and barbwire

we're setting up to serve breakfast
oatmeal and a piece of fruit
a styrofoam cup of milk
i'm positioned to keep
the flies off the food
a tradeoff as the hangar's
doors are open to let in
the cool morning air

orderly lines are formed
children first women second
then the men all nodding
their thanks while we keep
replacing the servings
as soon as they are taken
from the tables

huddled around the army green
cots called home during
the short time before
catching a bus or a train
i watch small families
eating and sharing a laugh
or young men off by themselves looking sullen
wishing for a cup of coffee
maybe some scrambled eggs

a visiting nurse from Albuquerque
points out a little boy
with curly brown hair

wearing a Spiderman t-shirt
and shorts who joyfully jumps
up and down
as his mother peels his orange

the nurse is smitten by his
innocent smile and squeals of delight
telling me he is "so cute"
while my thoughts are of children caged
in the neighboring state to the east
packed like sardines in small spaces
sleeping on concrete under mylar blankets
older kids becoming surrogate
mothers to the younger ones
children taking care of children
helpless and separated from their families
doing the best they can in the land of the free
where legal mouthpieces for a government
whose morals have become meaningless slogans
make the case in court that our democracy
is not required to provide showers, soap, and toothbrushes
to traumatized minors behind bars

looking at the carefree
little boy eating his orange
sticky juice dripping down his arms
my fellow volunteer seems
to be sharing my thoughts
"he's one of the lucky ones"

we walk outside without
saying a word

where articles of clothing
laundered in a small sink
hang listless along
the barb wire fence

and a row of port-a-potties
stand at attention

labor of love

the volunteer coordinator gives me a tour
of the makeshift processing center
an old airplane hangar converted
with Red Cross cots and folding chairs
a mish mash of computers on rickety plastic tables
pallets of bottled drinking water
occupying space in a corner of the building

asylum seekers dumped by the border patrol at 2 a.m.
in front of a McDonald's in a neighboring town are taken in
provided resources to find sponsors
a place to shower and rest
receive basic medical screenings
three meals a day
eventually given rides
to a bus station or airport

the older kids are kicking soccer balls
outside with some of my fellow volunteers
the little ones stay inside
sit in the roped off area just for them
busy with crayons, coloring books, and toys
a safe place where they return to being children
with their universal need to play

my first assigned job:
to sort through a mixed-up mess of donated clothing
a mountain of onesies, toddlers' Toy Story shorts,
XL men's t-shirts, ten yr old dresses from Sears,
and grandma's moldy Christmas sweaters

it's mundane but necessary work so i jump in
start separating by age and gender
becoming lost in the act of folding
i hardly notice the small figure kneeling beside me
age 6 or 7?

her delicate and nimble hands
hold up items from the pile
set aside for babies
each article of clothing inspected
with gentle care and reverence
my heart swells as she enacts motions
learned from who knows where
creating a tidy and meticulous
stack of infant wear

she looks up at me
a granddaughter i never had
her dark brown eyes meet mine
and ask if this is alright

while wondering about all the beauty
all the horror this precious
little being has witnessed
i nod my approval while wishing
my sparse and rarely used Spanish
vocabulary wasn't so elusive right now
then out of nowhere words come
"muy bien, mija"

smiling, she runs off
to rejoin her mother

we dance (after A.O.C.)

when we fold
warm sheets from the dryer
fabric stretched and pulled
between our moving figures
together stepping back
raising our arms and then
moving towards each other
slow and in synch
as the imperfect triangle
forms in our hands until
we are face to face
once again

when we drive
on the interstate
at night and the red lights
of the cars ahead begin
to float from one lane
to another then slow down
then speed up steady
and predictable
our instinct takes over
the trance of mind and body
reach out to the heavens
and joins the universe
expanding

when we walk
the crowded city streets
legs hips arms shoulders head
all move in rhythms embedded
long ago in our DNA
timid or bold
indifferent or cool
we saunter we stroll
individuals in a hive
of mass movement
the energy and heat
we create together
propelling us all
to the same
destination

a note to the young artists living in these dark days

go paint a picture in the rain
and watch the colors run or
write a poem while getting drunk
and listen to the random noise
of empty bottles breaking in the street
pick up a drum and beat it mad
as you dance naked in the backyard
under a suburban moon or drive
to the beach and sing jazz
to the stars hanging in a black
ink sky while wearing discarded
rags found in the trash bins
of local thrift stores or get
arrested for carving your visions
into the walls of public restrooms

know that the difference
between a dollar bill and
a sheet of toilet paper
is the green ink

close your eyes and
jump off the cliff
art will catch you

it always does

a rejection from Death

remember the time
i invited you in
thinking you would
ease my pain
just a kid in high school
heart-broken and ready
to give it up

farewell letters written
i swallowed half the sleeping
pills in the package
curled up on the motel
bed and waited for you
to come with your
saccharine kiss and lift
the hurt crushing my chest

hours later
woke up
somehow knew
the sounds of
early morning traffic
should not be a part

of the afterlife and
the dead probably
don't have to piss
first thing in the
morning

on the way home
stopped at Denny's
sat by a window
watched a crow
picking at something
furry and lying still
in the street
ordered breakfast

their shitty coffee
never tasted so good

64th winter, a birthday poem

then,
a cloud of cold air rushed
into newborn lungs and stifled
the cry stuck in my throat
eyes opened wide
the life presented to me
was a box of rusty nails
spilled across a muddy road

now,
an old crow perches
on a weathered wooden pole
strung with sagging barbed wire
he flaps his wings
caws in my direction
its harsh sound softened
by the layer of white
that blankets the hard
ground as far as i can see

iv.

A Father's Gift

I have a list of "firsts" stored in my memory. Age three, I threw up my first slice of pizza. Age seven, my first bicycle, a beat-up hand-me-down my mom picked up at a police auction for five bucks. And at age thirteen, my first French kiss with one of the "A" list girls at Hosler Jr. High. She cornered me under the mistletoe, definitely one of my prouder moments. But right up there, at the top of the list, I must include the one time I came close enough to reach out and touch the white powder my father injected into his arms. I was only four years old.

He pulled the car into the driveway, already regretting not shooting up in the garage where he had purchased the heroin. When he sat down and pulled out his kit, the guy who sold it to him said he had some business to attend to, and he would have to go somewhere else. Now he would have to shoot up at the house. Sitting in the comfort of his backyard or the privacy of his bedroom and smoking a joint was one thing. Closing the door, locking it, preparing a syringe, and sticking it into his vein, while his wife and kids were in the next room watching TV, was another matter. The thought made him feel uncomfortable.

The smell of carne cooked in red chile, rice, fresh beans, and homemade flour tortillas greeted him as he walked through the door, but the aching chill in his bones was getting worse, growing into a desperate and more demanding appetite he could not put off for much longer.

"My daddy's a cowboy," I used to proclaim to my classmates in kindergarten. Watching him roll his own cigarettes with the pungent tobacco he kept in a shoebox is one of my favorite childhood memories. He would sprinkle the dried weed into the course, yellowed paper, roll it between his fingers, and then with one fluid motion, swipe the tip of his tongue along the glued edge. I had watched John Wayne do the same thing a hundred times in the movies, but he had nothing over my father.

Our other ritual was the washing of the car, every Saturday morning. The chrome was polished till it sparkled in the warm, midmorning sun, and I could see my reflection in the baby blue paint job. Then I would climb in on the passenger side and, in a time before seat belts, standup and hold on as we took the car for a cruise; my slick lowrider father and his mijito driving slowly through the streets of downtown Compton. He rolled up the windows and lit one of his special cigarettes. The cloud of secondhand smoke did not smell harsh like regular cigarette smoke but was sweet and pleasurable as it filled my little lungs. Everything slowed down to a crawl, and the shop windows displaying women's shoes and the mannequins wearing the latest fashions drifted by like a hazy summer dream. The sounds of Ray Charles or Bobby Darin played on the radio as my father's friends pulled up alongside us at the red light, their dark hair combed back slick and shiny from greasy gobs of Tres Flores pomade. Information was passed back and forth about the weekend's parties and dances, which girls would be where, and who scored what. Then they nodded in my direction, "Shit, Richard. He looks just like you, ese. Hey, little man, you doin' alright? You keeping your old man in line?" They would laugh as the light changed and pull ahead to the next familiar car on the road, collecting and disseminating news about the neighborhood like a switchboard on wheels.

His son and his two daughters were playing in the backyard. They came running when they heard his car pull up. He knelt to hug his babies, opening his lunch box and pulling out three Tootsie Rolls. They kissed their father on the cheek and heard their mother call out from the kitchen, telling them the candy was for after dinner. He sank down into the secondhand easy chair with the tattered upholstery in the sparsely furnished living room. His children started untying his work boots, tugging, and pulling until they finally came off his sweaty feet. All the time he kept thinking about the balloon of white powder in his pocket calling out his name... "Richard! Richard! I'm right here, baby. What are you waiting for?"

After dinner, he locked himself in the bathroom, unpacked his kit, and focused on what he had to do. The plan was to get high in the bathroom then retreat to the bedroom for the rest of the night. There would be no family time tonight, no "Bugs Bunny Show," no bowl of popcorn drenched in melted butter as they all huddled around on the floor, crunching in unison, and laughing at the antics of Bugs, Yosemite Sam, and Daffy Duck.

Tonight, was his night to spend in his other world, alone.

I was a month shy of starting the first grade. I can remember the Friday night our mother loaded us up in the car and took us to the drive-in, without him. It was payday. There were groceries to buy. Mouths to feed. Where in the hell was he? I knew she was upset when I heard her say aloud to no one, "Let him come home to a dark and empty house, goddamnit," as she backed the car into the street.

Upon returning home, the headlights of the car swept across the front yard as it turned into the driveway, lighting up the figure of my father face down, passed out on the cold, wet lawn. Our mother jumped out of the car, knelt at his side, lifted his head, leaned in close to make sure he was breathing, and slapped him hard to wake him up.

We were still in the car looking out the windows, wondering why our father was sleeping outside. We watched our mother try to lift him up. She called out to me, told me to go next door and get help. I ran to our neighbor's house and knocked on the door. He answered, took one look at our dilemma, and ran over to give us a hand. Without saying a word, he helped lift our father off the ground and carry him into the house. They sat him down at the kitchen table. We were rushed off to bed, as our mother stayed up the rest of the night, nursing her husband back from the brink.

He had poured the contents of the balloon into the measuring spoon and was going to add drops of water when he heard feet dancing on the other side of the door. The hunger inside was gnawing at him, and the only thing he needed was so close. "Daddy, I have to pee!" Through the sharp pain wracking his brain, he heard the urgency in the boy's plea. His five-year-old son had no idea what he was going through. The only thing that mattered was his son had to pee, now. He heard the doorknob as it jiggled back and forth. The dancing noises were getting frantic. He took off the leather belt around his arm's bulging vein, picked up the implements of his habit, and stashed them behind the shower curtain in the corner of the tub. He unlocked the door and opened it. His son ran in, pulled his pants down around his ankles, aimed his penis for the center of the bowl, then let out an "Ahhhhh..."

He closed the door and waited in the hallway.

I once witnessed my father getting arrested. I was not in school at the time, so I will say it was the summer between ages four and five. I was home watching my favorite afternoon cartoon, Tom and Jerry. The front door was open because we had a screen door. I heard a knock, and although I knew better than to talk to strangers, I went to see who it was. Standing on our porch were two white men. I stared at this odd couple. The one at the door trying to peer

111

in from the other side of the screen as his partner was scanning the outside of our house. He was looking for something. White people did not live where we lived. We did not know any, except for the man whose car was parked in my aunt's driveway every Friday and Saturday night. His name was Mike, and the grownups in the family did not like to talk about him.

The men at my door were dressed funny. One of them was wearing a denim jacket and jeans. The other was dressed in a black jacket, white t-shirt, and jeans. The white men I saw on TV always wore shirts and ties, and when they got home from work, they slipped on a cardigan sweater, slippers, and smoked pipes in the study while reading the newspaper. Their wives wore clean, crisp house dresses, and they called each other "dear." The white men always wore pajamas at bedtime, and they and their wives always slept in separate beds. The fact that my parents slept in one bed, not two, was one more way I thought white people were better than us.

"Hi, sonny. Is your dad home?"

Snapped from my spell, I turned around to look for my mother. There she was, standing behind me. She directed me back to my cartoons, then told the men she did not know where my father was or when he would be home. She closed the door, and less than a minute later, we heard noises coming from the backyard. We went to the kitchen and opened the backdoor. He was between the men, his arms handcuffed behind his back. They had found him hiding in the garage. Neighbors from all sides of our backyard were peering over the fence. He saw me and told my mother to take me back inside. For a moment, our eyes met as if we were saying goodbye, and then he was gone.

My childhood transformed into a blur of memories; weekend visits to various jails or the men's state prison in Chino, and always remembering to reply that my father was in the navy and out to sea whenever strangers asked of his whereabouts.

His release created a different scenario. Unannounced nighttime visits by tired-looking parole officers, who asked a lot of questions and took notes as my parents smiled a lot. They tried to look so happy it was scary. As they introduced me, my sisters, and my baby brother, we must have looked like props, pieces on a set to convince the parole officer we were trying to be a normal American family.

There were also the regular Friday night appointments at the methadone clinic. After the family trip to the market, stocking up on the week's supply of groceries, we all took a ride to the clinic. We sat in a dark parking lot, waiting for half an hour. My mother told us our father had an appointment to see a doctor, and he was getting better. He always came back to us a more mellowed and subdued man.

Eventually, it got better for us. My father got hired on as an apprentice welder. He was learning a trade and making decent money. The surprise visits from parole officers faded away. The weekly appointments at the clinic finally ended.

I knew we were turning a corner the day I got a brand-new bike. My police auction special was on its last legs, but I had never complained. Then, one day my father came home from work and said, "Let's go for a ride. Just you and me." He took me to a bicycle shop and asked me which one I liked. I knew which bike I liked the minute we walked in; it had a banana seat and biker handlebars. The paint job was a sparkly gold metal flake. It was not the Schwinn Stingray all my friends rode, but I did not care. It had taken me 9 years to get one; I finally had my first brand new bicycle.

Christmas that year was the best. We had a real tree flocked with fake snow. I would sit and stare at the colored lights flashing in the dark. I never tired looking at my distorted reflection peering back at me from the globe-shaped red and green glass ornaments. The smell of pine filled my nostrils, and I knew this was a real Christmas, at last. And the presents! They were stacked higher than I could ever hope or dream. Christmas morning was one continuous shout of glee as we unwrapped Barbies and doll houses and G.I. Joes and toy tanks and skates and puzzles and board games and plastic models of my favorite monsters (Frankenstein and the Wolfman) and even a small airplane with a real gas motor to propel it through the air.

Everything was better and new. It was only a matter of time before we took our place alongside the other families who had the latest model of station wagons and houses with white picket fences, who took summer vacations and did things together. The struggle was over, gone like a bad dream. Only good times were ahead. Or so it seemed.

A few weeks later, on January 16, 1965, I woke up to my mother shaking me, telling me to get up and get dressed. It was a Saturday, and I pulled the covers over myhead. It was a game we played. Then she would sing to me, belt some god-awful song she made up on the spot. Since she could not carry a tune to save her life (a trait I've unfortunately inherited) I would stick my fingers in my ears and plead for her to stop. But there was no singing asI heard her going from one bunk bed to the next, shaking my sisters and brother, directing all of us to wake up.

I threw the covers back and saw my father's only brother. My uncle stood in the doorway, head down, as tears rolled down his cheeks. My mother's eyes were red, and she looked like she had been crying for a long time. Then she announced in a low, calm voice, "Your father is dead." I wish I could say she held me and gave me comfort as I burst into tears, but I cannot.

Later, I found out he had been hanging out with his old friends, slipping back into his old habits. On this night, he had scored some heroin that had not been cut right. It was purer than the usual drug on the streets. He immediately overdosed. A lot of time was wasted because almost everyone involved was on probation or on parole, and an incident like this had legal ramifications that could send people back to jail. He was dropped off with some other friends from the old neighborhood, who drove him home. My mother left us alone, asleep in the house, as she rushed him to the emergency room in the early morning hours.

While my mother sat next to my father in the ER and waited for medical attention, a doctor passing by stopped, took one look at my father slumped over in the chair, took his pulse, and said casually, "This man is dead."

The week that followed was another series of blurs. I vaguely remember sitting in my grandmother's kitchen, as my father's brother talked about going across town and confronting some people, and my grandfather telling him how foolish and dangerous that would be. I remember that the funeral home always had fresh donuts from Winchell's. I remember the matching dark green sweaters and black slacks my brother and I had to wear to the funeral and how the coarse material of the sweater made me itch. I remember the thick, nauseous smell of too many flower arrangements in one room. I remember the new lie we were coached to tell whenever asked how our 29-year-old father had died, "My dad had a heart attack."

And I remember this as if it were yesterday: I was five years old, jumping up and down in the hallway, begging my father to open the bathroom door and let me use the toilet. He unlocked the door and let me in. I made a beeline for the bowl, pulling my pants down around my ankles, standing on my tiptoes, and taking aim. He stepped out and closed the door as the splash of my pee sounded like music to my ears. I began to look around, taking note of my surroundings, when I saw it. On the corner of the tub, partially hidden behind the shower curtain. I had enough doctor visits to know what it was. The needle could only mean one thing, my father was sick. I did not understand my mother's measuring spoon and the white powder it held. Even more confusing was the blue balloon. Did the doctor run out of candy suckers? I finished my business, pulled up my pants, and opened the door. He was standing there, waiting.

Why I never said a word to anyone, I will never know.

One thing was certain, my childhood was taken from me that day. I know some will read this and roll their eyes. *Christ! Another writer whining about his tragic and pitiful life. Can't these people find anything else to write about?* I have, and I do. But what I have come to realize is no one has the perfect childhood. We spend a lifetime trying to unfuck ourselves, recover from the sins of our mothers and fathers, and then turn around and hope we do not do the same to our own kids.

I grew up hating my father. The choice was simple, heroin or me. He chose heroin. The bitterness poisoned my heart. The sense of rejection tainted my relationships. I pushed people away or left them before they could leave me. Some people have a hard time with it, but I never had a problem saying, "I love you." It is easy when you don't really know what it means. From the time I was a teen, I knew that I did not want to have children, a promise I have kept to myself all these years.

It was not until thirty years after his death, during the mandatory midlife crisis and the ensuing therapy sessions, that I revisited my past, looking for answers. Catching up with strangers who cut me off on the road for the simple satisfaction of giving them the finger, confronting coworkers over the most insignificant thing and hoping someone would throw a punch, family gatherings that always fell apart once my sisters found something to scream and argue about, a brother who casually left his wife and one-year-old daughter when he got his best friend's wife pregnant, and an insecure mother who didn't care what her current husband sold to raise the illegal money needed to pay for their comfortable lifestyle were all too much. I was looking for the source, and all arrows pointed at my father.

My therapist asked and probed, and I recalled most of the memories I have already written about. But she kept pushing me, helping me remember things I had blocked out over the years. One memory stood out from the rest: I am shivering under the covers of my bed, shaking uncontrollably as the chills overtake my small, eight-year-old body. My teeth chatter. I am waiting for my mother to return from the store with urgently needed over-the-counter medicine. We cannot afford a doctor. I turn my head and see him standing in the doorway. The light from the hallway behind him creates a dark silhouette. I cannot see his face. He walks into the room, bends over me, and tucks the blankets around me, snug and tight. He puts his rough hand on my forehead and my cheek, trying to gauge my fever. He does not say a word. Then he lies down next to me, holding me close. He is taking deep, deliberate breaths. I can hear and feel his heartbeat. His body heat begins to wrap around me, heating up the blankets, until I am in a warm cocoon and the shivering has stopped. My breathing naturally synchronizes with his, and my eyes close. Before I doze off, the last thing I remember is feeling safe and loved.

And this is how I finally realized my father loved me and never stopped loving me. The demon he battled had nothing to do with me. But it could have. That night so long ago, while I stood in the bathroom, peeing, it had made its presence known to me; smiled and winked as if we were destined to become close friends.

My father was a heroin addict. It was his struggle, and it had nothing to do with me. I like to think, somehow, he knew his early exit would make sure it stayed that way.

And in my mind, this is the only truth that matters.

AUTHOR'S BIOGRAPHY

Richard Vargas earned his B.A. at Cal State University, Long Beach, where he studied under Gerald Locklin and Richard Lee. He edited/ published five issues of *The Tequila Review*, 1978-1980, and twelve issues of *The Más Tequila Review* from 2010-2015. Vargas received his MFA in Creative Writing from the University of New Mexico, 2010. He was recipient of the 2011 Taos Summer Writers' Conference Hispanic Writer Award. He was on the faculties of the 2012 10th National Latino Writers Conference and the 2015 Taos Summer Writers' Conference. Published collections: *McLife*, 2005; *American Jesus*, 2009; *Guernica, revisited*, 2014, and a new collection of poems scheduled for publication in Summer 2022. He currently resides in Wisconsin, near the lake where Otis Redding's plane crashed.

www.ingramcontent.com/pod-product-compliance
Lightning Source LLC
Chambersburg PA
CBHW070312120726
47910CB00007B/2452